KU-111-863

GEOMETRY WITH A TANGRAM

GEOMETRY WITH A TANGRAM

David Fletcher &
Joseph Ibbotson

Foreword: Prof. F. W. Land

CREDITS

Devised by David Fletcher and Joseph Ibbotsen.

Art: Based upon design by

Fred Gettings, of Saint John's Art Consultants, Oxford.

Set in 12 Didot Univers with titling in Albertus.

Printed in lithography by George Outram & Co. Ltd., Aberdeen.

Published by W & R Holmes Ltd., Glasgow.

Copyright © W & R Holmes Ltd., 1965.

FOREWORD

This is one of a series of books which have been designed for use in junior schools. The material introduced has been used by children for several years and the form in which it is presented here is the result of much exploratory work on the part of the authors.

Tangrams are nothing but simple shapes designed to fit together in many different ways. When they are well made and colourful they invite children to invent shapes for themselves, to use their imaginations, and to exercise their ingenuity in fitting pieces together. This book includes many illustrations which suggest ways of fitting the pieces together but, although these illustrations do give plenty of ideas and indications of how tangrams may be used, they are only illustrations and suggestions. The real value of the material is that children can make shapes and patterns for themselves. The book also indicates how some of the shapes and patterns can be compared and how they illustrate ideas about symmetry or area and about special shapes such as squares, rectangles, parallelograms or triangles. When children have made shapes which they think are pleasing or interesting they can be encouraged to talk about them and find out more about them.

Tangrams provide a variety of experiences; children get used to shapes and sizes, use their judgment in selecting pieces which will fit and in this way build up their background. At a later stage they will be doing more formal geometry and this will be so much richer because of the way in which they have obtained all this experience of shape, size and pattern and of

FOREWORD Contd.

the practice they give themselves in careful observation. At the age when they should be playing with tangrams, children are at what Piaget describes as the stage of concrete operations. They can make two triangles using different tangram pieces and actually place one on the top of the other and see that one exactly fits on top of the other and, by actually doing the operation of fitting, can experience the fact that the two shapes are congruent. They can use this word. The children will not meet formal geometry for some years but when they do have to understand the abstract idea of congruence they will have had the benefit of a variety of actual experiences from which to abstract this important concept. When using tangrams they come face to face with parallels and angles, figures with different shapes but the same area, figures with similar shapes and different areas and so on. These experiences will be most valuable to them provided the teacher lets the children explore for themselves, encourages talk about the shapes which have been made, using the right words such as congruent, similar, parallel, area, isosceles triangle or what ever is appropriate, but resists the temptation to introduce formalised geometry which belongs to a later stage of development.

These tangrams are meant to be enjoyed, they are only an incident in junior school mathematics and children should be given something quite different to work with long before they show any signs of becoming bored with tangrams.

F. W. Land

CONTENTS

The Tangram

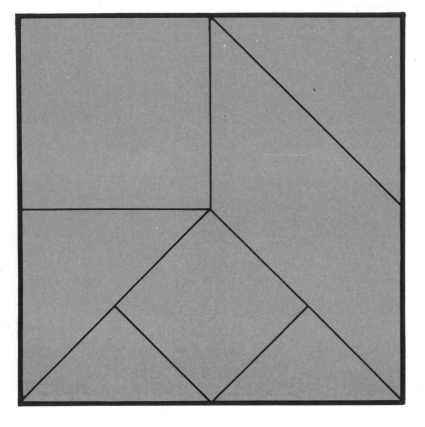

Two Squares

Two Small Triangles

Two Large Triangles

One Parallelogram

There are seven pieces making up the Tangram. On pages 8 to 11 there are six different shapes. It is possible to make these shapes using five, six or seven pieces of the Tangram. How many of them can you make?

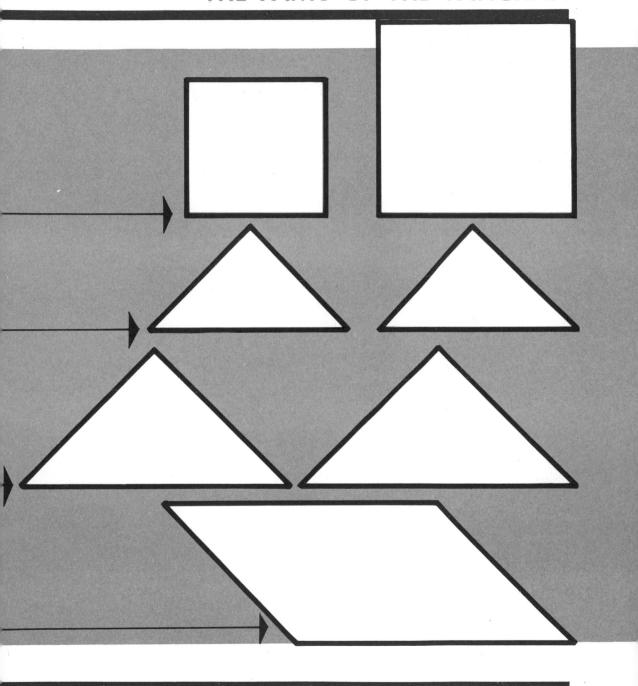

MAKING SHAPES

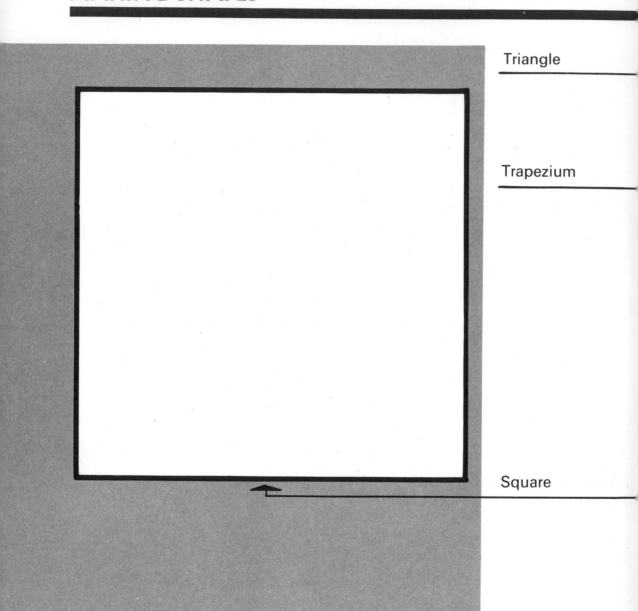

Triangle

Trapezium

Square

Making Shapes

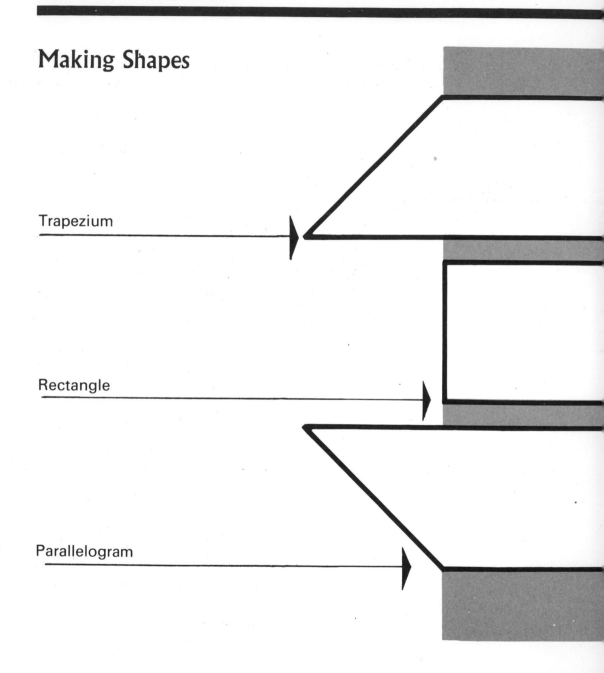

Trapezium

Rectangle

Parallelogram

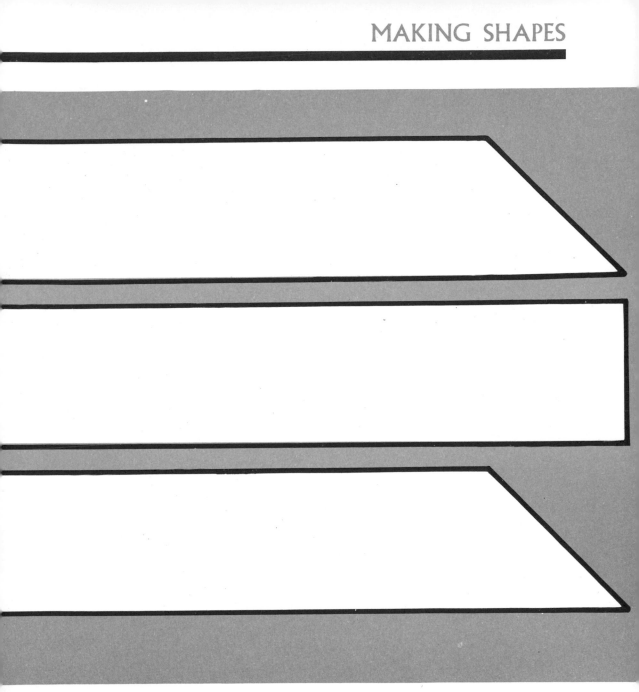

Making Triangles

What is a triangle? Do you know the names of any special kinds of triangles?

1.   Make two triangles using two pieces for each triangle. Are the two triangles the same size? If not, how do they differ?

2.   Using each piece once only, make two triangles so that there are three pieces in each triangle.

3.   Find some other ways of making triangles using three pieces.

4.   How many triangles can you make using four pieces only?

5.   Make some triangles which contain five pieces.

6.   Is it possible to make a triangle using six pieces only?

7.   Use all seven pieces to make a triangle.

8.   (a)   Make one triangle using

       Two small triangles
       One large triangle
       The Parallelogram

(b) Now change the triangle you have just made into a rectangle by moving one piece only.

(c) Change the triangle into a rectangle by moving two pieces.

Making Rectangles

What is a rectangle? Why is a rectangle a special kind of parallelogram? How can you test whether a shape is a rectangle or not?

Exploration

When you have found the answers to the following questions, make sketches to record your answers.

1. Make the smallest rectangle you can, and then find a second way of making one which is equal to it in area.

2. From the seven pieces build two rectangles.

3. How many rectangles can you make using any three pieces?

4. Using four pieces make a rectangle. In how many different ways can you do this?

5. Make a rectangle using five pieces. Can you find more than one way of doing this?

6. Make a rectangle using six pieces. Record your results.

7. Using all seven pieces, make a rectangle in as many ways as possible.

8. Using the parallelogram and the four triangles make a shape which looks like two rectangles crossing each other.

Making Squares

What is a square? How can you test whether a shape is a square or not?

Exploration

1. Make a square using two pieces.
2. Make another square using two different pieces.
3. Make a square using three pieces.
4. Is it possible to make a square using:
   (a) Any four pieces?
   (b) Any five pieces?
5. Make four squares using six pieces of the Tangram.
6. Make a square using all seven pieces of the Tangram.
7. What does *perimeter* mean?
8. Find the perimeter of each of the squares you have made.

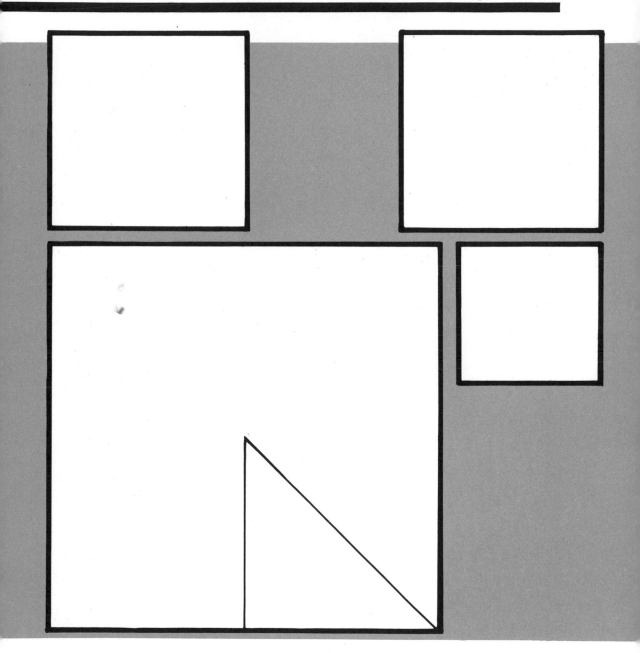

Making Parallelograms

What is a parallelogram? Why is a rectangle a special kind of parallelogram?

Exploration

When you have found the answers to the following questions make sketches to record the answers.

1. Arrange the seven pieces so that they make three parallelograms.

2. How many different parallelograms can you make using three pieces?

3. There are several ways of making parallelograms with four pieces. How many can you discover?

4. Parallelograms can be made using five pieces. Record the answers you find.

5. Use six pieces and make as many parallelograms as possible.

6. Use all seven pieces and make a parallelogram.

7. Make a parallelogram and, by moving one piece, change it into a rectangle. Do this with parallelograms of different sizes.

8. Is it necessary to use all the pieces to make the longest parallelogram?

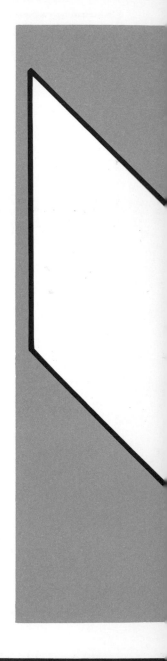

Making Trapeziums

A trapezium is a four-sided figure with two sides parallel.

Here are two kinds of trapezium:

This is an isosceles trapezium. See how it fits into an isosceles triangle.

This is a right-angled trapezium. Notice how it fits into a right-angled triangle.

Is it possible to make an isosceles trapezium using 2, 3, 4, 5, 6 or 7 pieces?
Is it possible to make a right-angled trapezium using 2, 3, 4, 5, 6 or 7 pieces?

Naming the Pieces

Each piece is named by using initial letters. The parallelogram, for example, is called P.

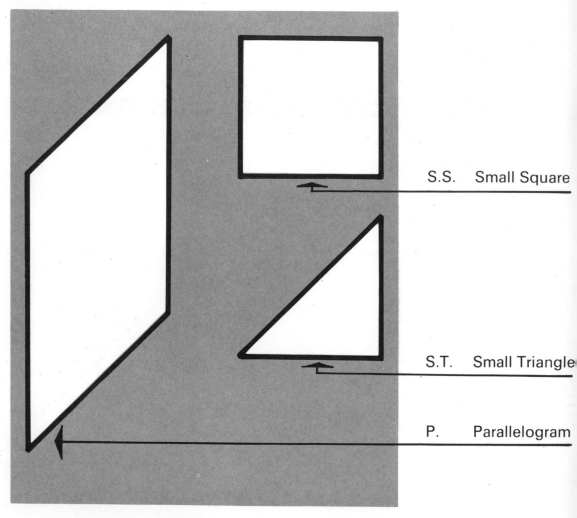

S.S.   Small Square

S.T.   Small Triangle

P.   Parallelogram

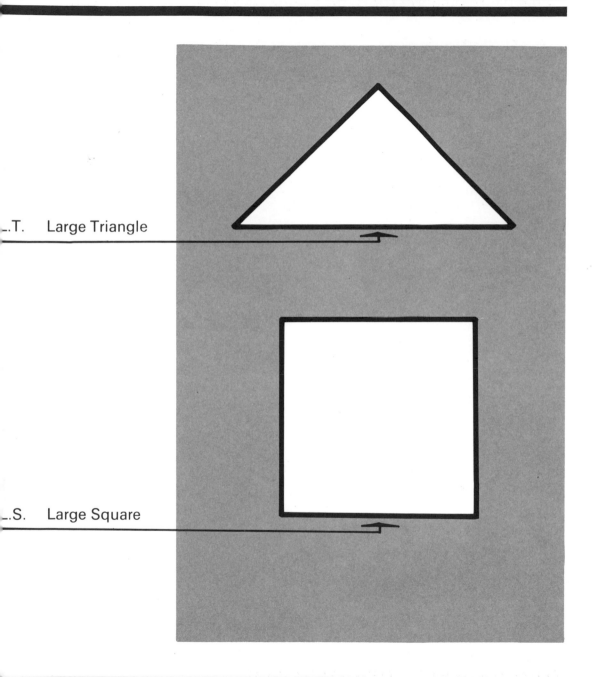

L.T.   Large Triangle

L.S.   Large Square

Making Shapes

On the following fifteen pages are a number of shapes. Make these shapes using the pieces indicated, and then make drawings to show how you have put the pieces together. The one on the next page has been done for you.

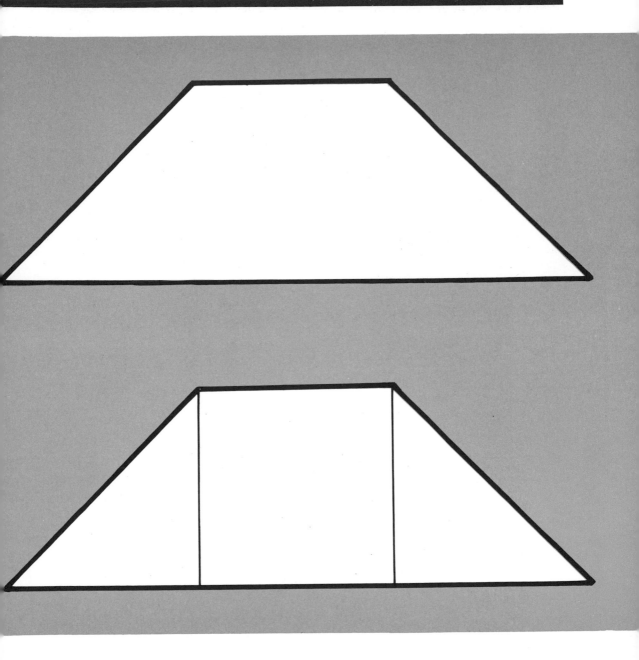

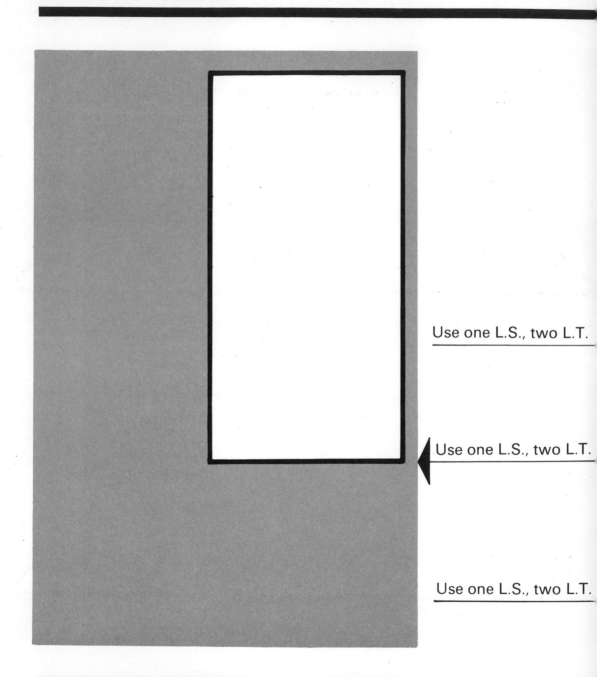

Use one L.S., two L.T.

Use one L.S., two L.T.

Use one L.S., two L.T.

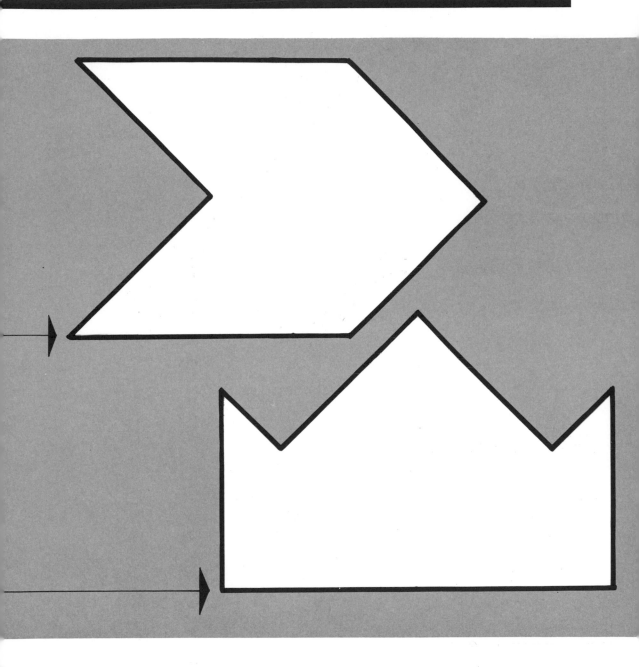

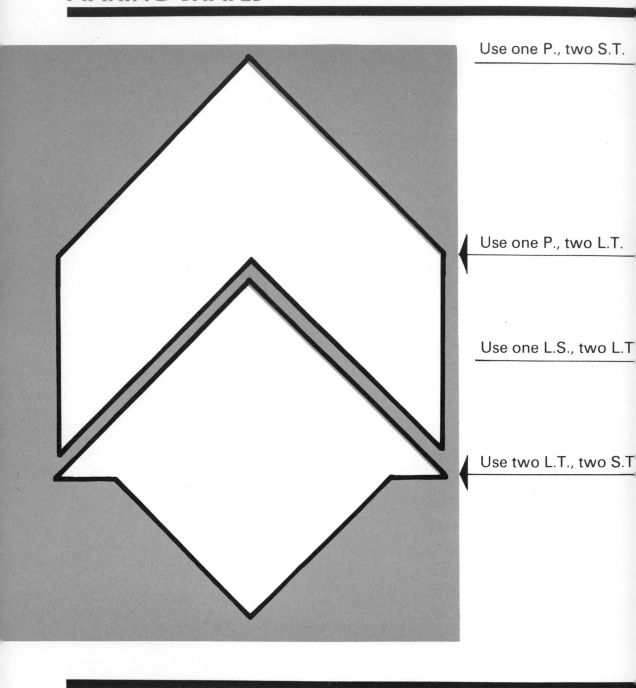

Use one P., two S.T.

Use one P., two L.T.

Use one L.S., two L.T

Use two L.T., two S.T

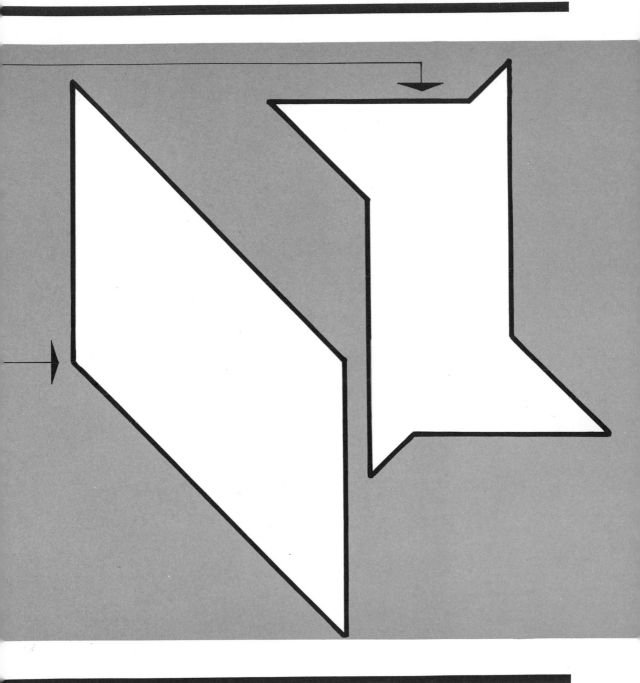

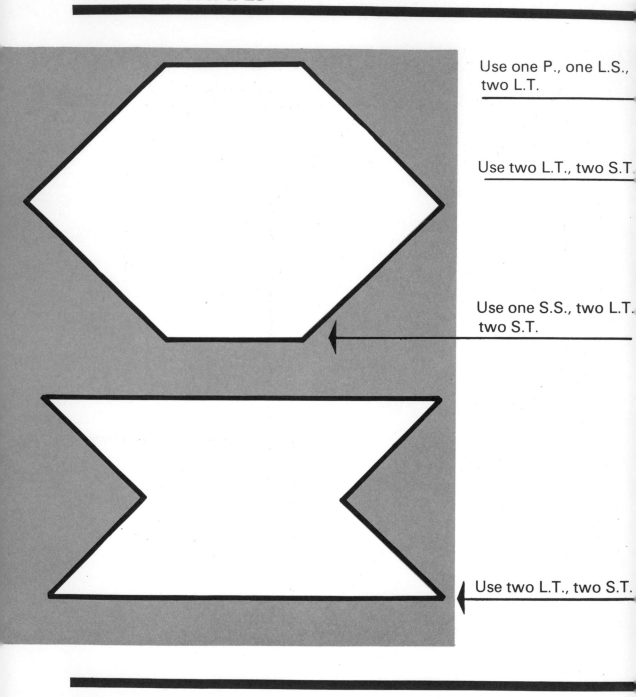

Use one P., one L.S., two L.T.

Use two L.T., two S.T.

Use one S.S., two L.T. two S.T.

Use two L.T., two S.T.

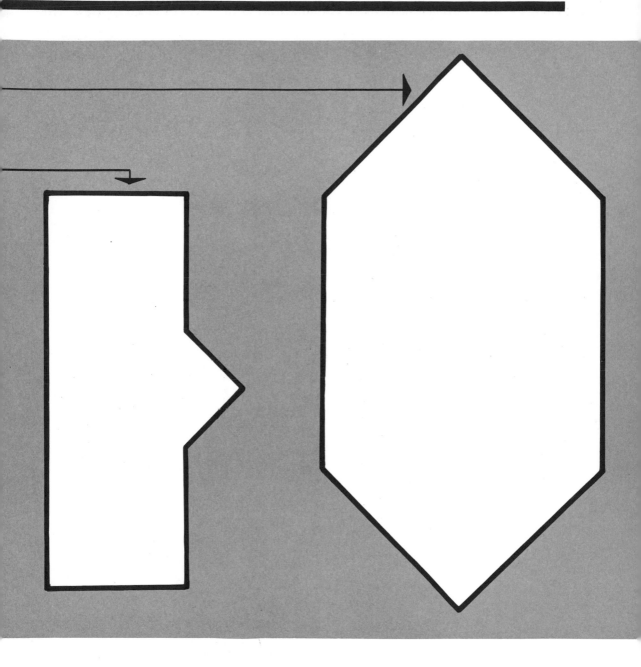

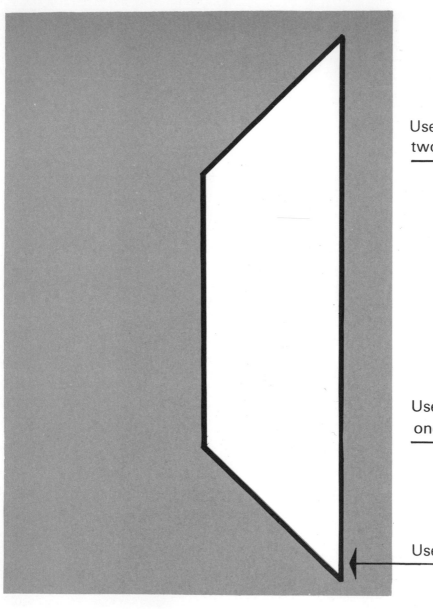

Use one P., one L.T., two S.T.

Use one P., one L.T., one S.S., two S.T.

Use one P., one L.T.

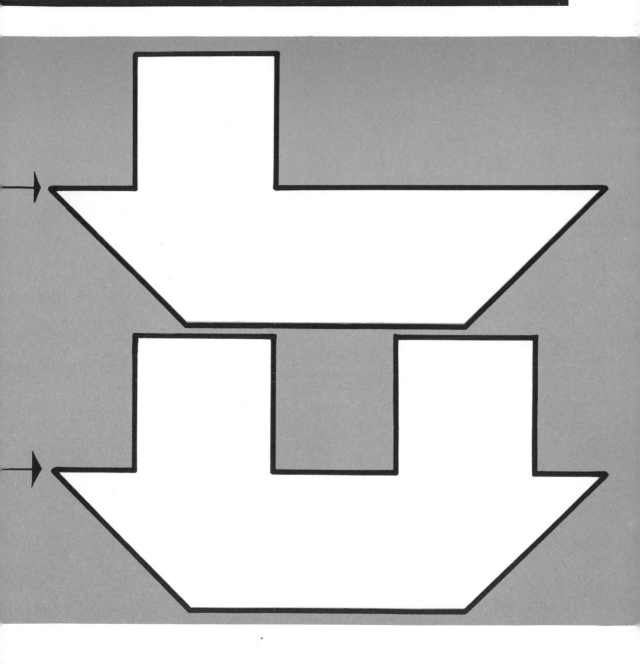

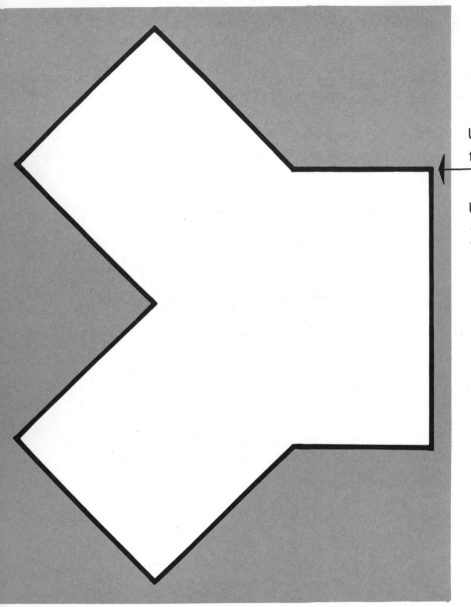

Use one P., one L.S.,
two L.T., two S.T.

Use one P., two L.T.
two S.T.

Use one L.S., two L.T

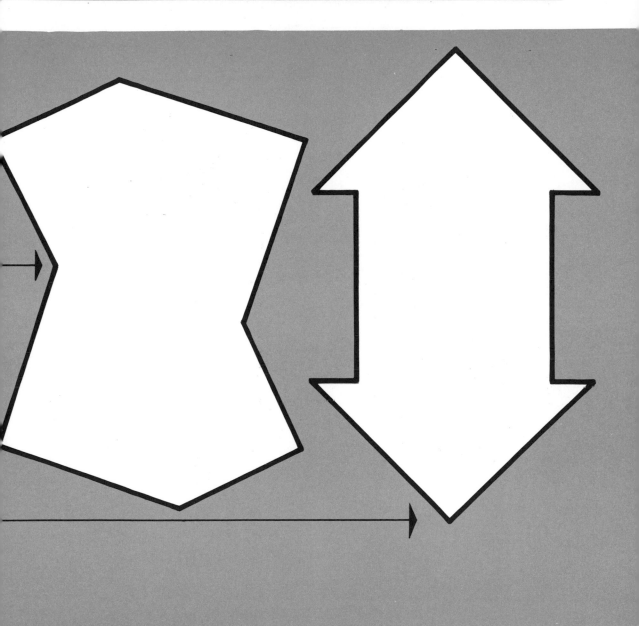

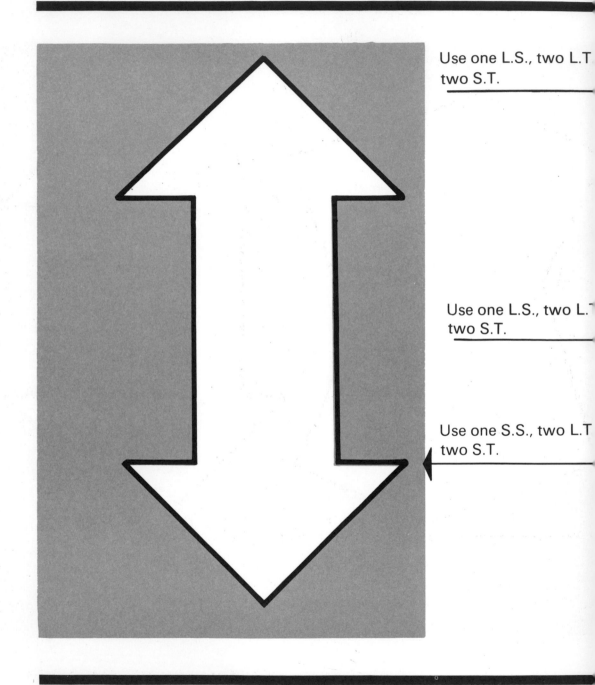

Use one L.S., two L.T
two S.T.

Use one L.S., two L.T
two S.T.

Use one S.S., two L.T
two S.T.

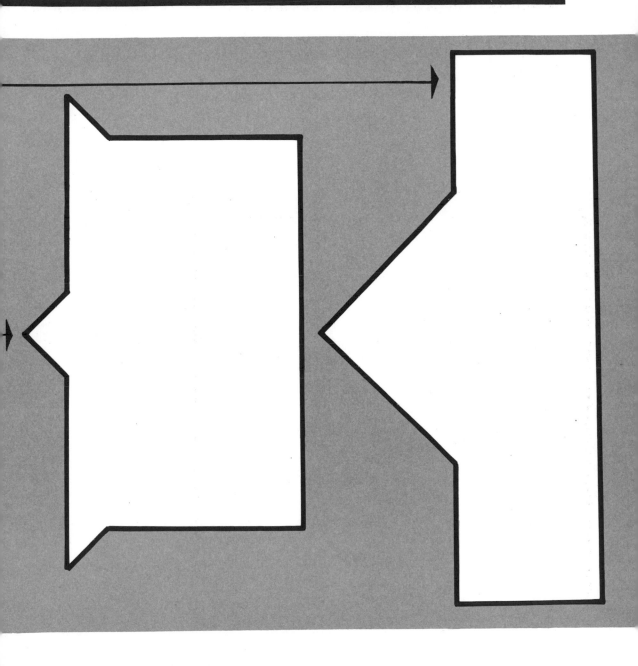

Making Shapes

Now try making some more shapes of your own design. Ask your partner to copy your shapes and say which pieces were used.

Use all the seven pieces to make a square.

Use one L.S., one P two S.T.

Use one P., two L.T

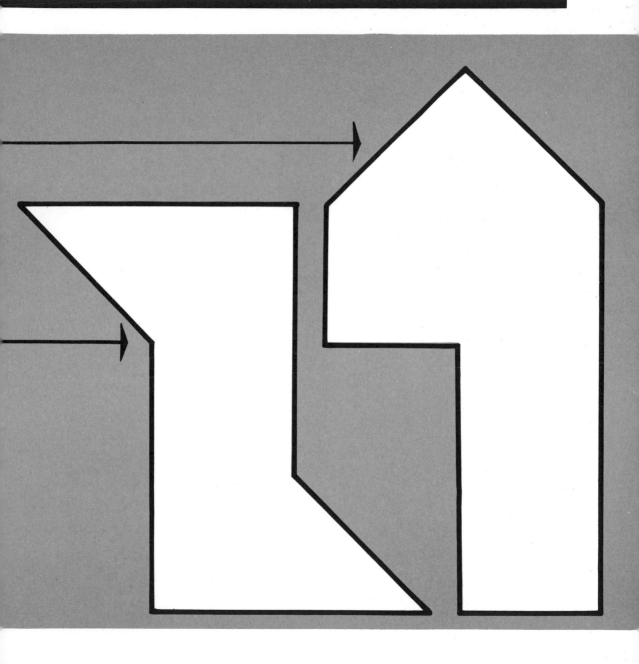

Area

What is meant by area? How is area measured?
Put the large square on your desk. What is the length
of one side? What is the perimeter of the square?
From squared paper, cut out some 1 inch squares
and find out how many are required to cover the
large square.

Exploration

1. What is the area of the large square?
2. Fit the two large triangles over the large square.
What is the area of one large triangle?
3. Using two large triangles, find the area of the
parallelogram.
4. Fit the two small triangles over the large triangle.
What is the area of one of the small triangles?
5. Place the two small triangles on the small square.
What is the area of the small square?

Area

What is the area of each of the following shapes?
The Parallelogram. The Large Triangle. The Small
Triangle. The Small Square. The Large Square.
What is the total area of the seven pieces?

1 Parallelogram	_____	sq. in
2 Large Triangles	_____	sq. in
2 Small Triangles	_____	sq. in
1 Small Square	_____	sq. in
1 Large Square	_____	sq. in
TOTAL AREA	_____	sq. in

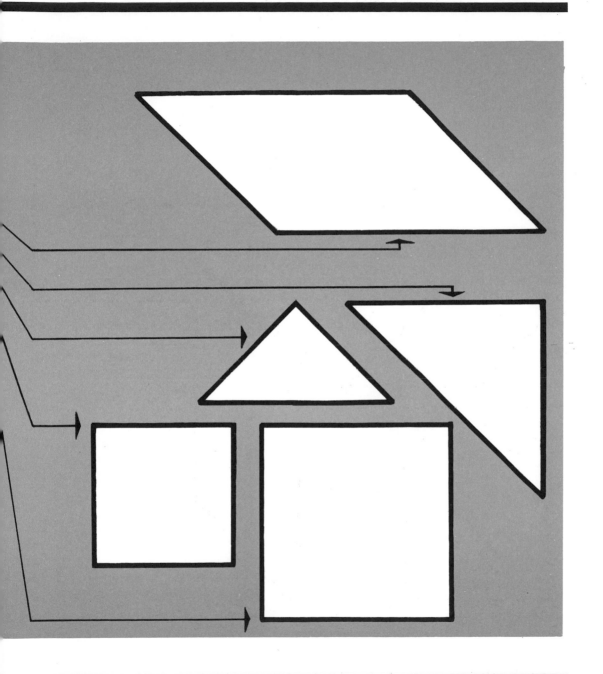

Area

On the following four pages are shapes made by combining *two* or *three* of the seven pieces.

When you have discovered how each of the shapes is made, sketch it and write down the area. Some shapes can be made in two sizes.

Area

Make the following shapes, and write down the area of each one.

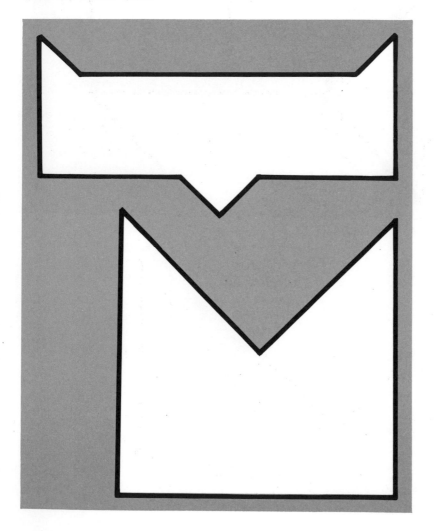

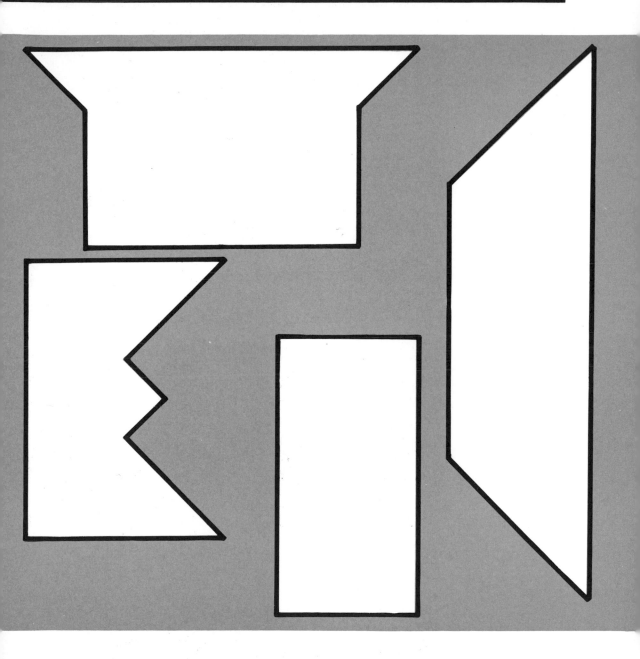

Area

When answering the following questions, first build the shape and then make a sketch of it.

1.   How many different shapes can you discover which have an area equal to that of:
  (a)   the large square?
  (b)   the small square?

2.   Look at this shape. Find its area, and make as many shapes as you can which have the same area. ━━━━━   ━━

3.   What is the area of this shape? Make ten more shapes with the same area.   ━━━━━━━━━━

4.   Make this shape. Find it's area, and make ten more shapes which are equal in area.   ━━━━━━━━━

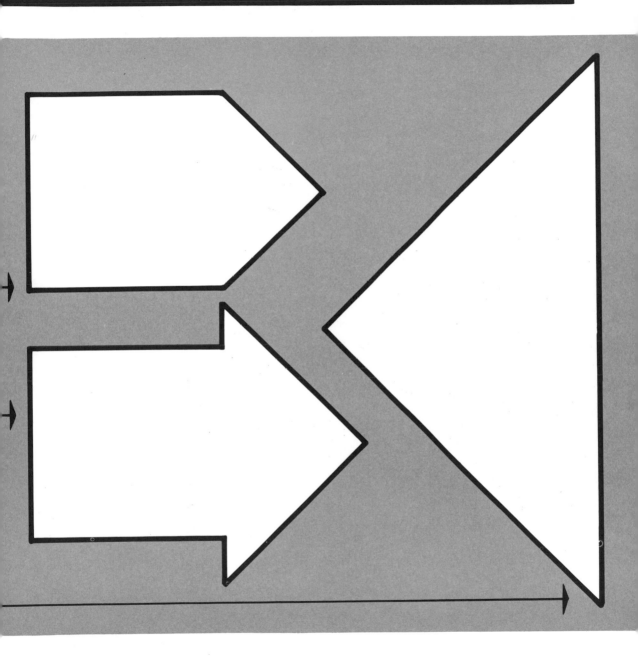

Rearrangements – Triangles

The area of both the triangle and the parallelogram can be found by first changing the shape into that of a rectangle.

Make the two triangles on these two pages and then, by moving the necessary pieces, change them into rectangles.

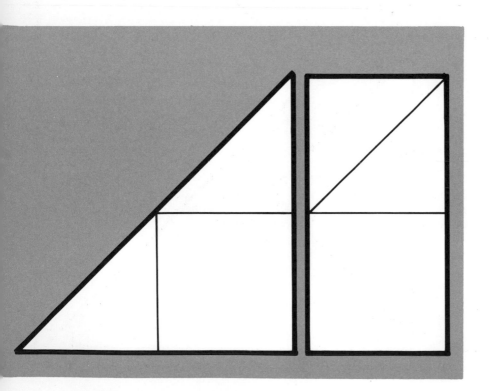

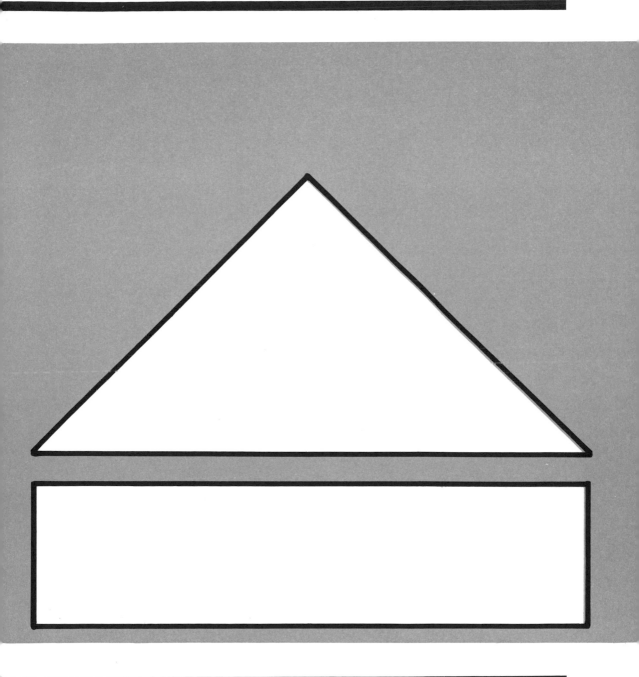

Rearrangements – Parallelograms

Make the parallelograms on these two pages, and then, by moving the necessary pieces, change them into rectangles. What are their areas?

Making and changing these shapes will help you to discover a simple rule which will help you to find the area of all triangles and parallelograms.

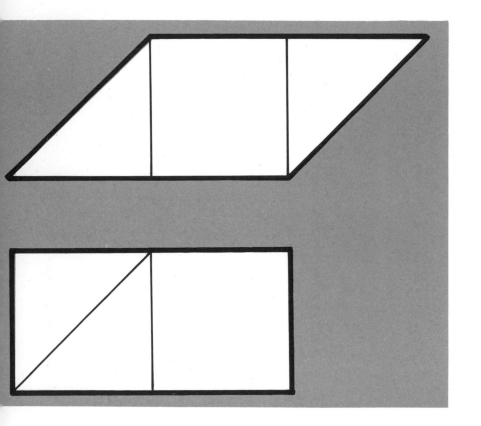

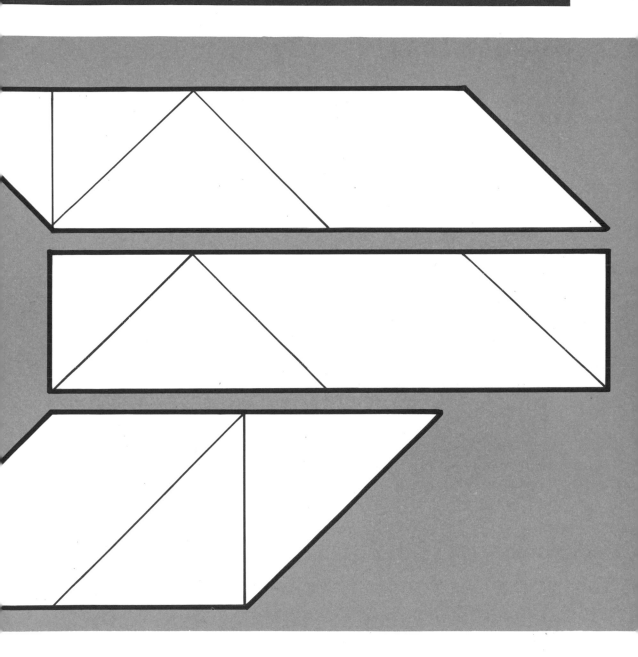

Area

Make a rectangle using the pieces shown below.

1. Find the length of the rectangle.
2. Find the height of the rectangle.
3. What is its area?

Change the position of one piece to make the rectangle into a triangle.

4. Find the length of the base of the triangle.
5. Find the height of the triangle.
6. What is the area of the triangle?

Move one piece and transform the triangle into a parallelogram.

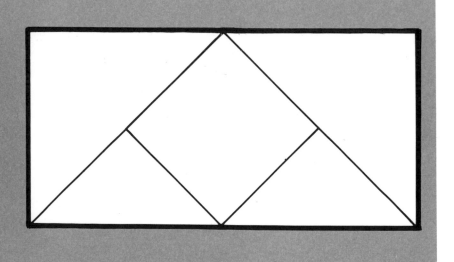

Area

7.   Find the length of the parallelogram.

8.   Find the height of the parallelogram.

9.   What is its area?

Change the position of one piece of this parallelogram to make a trapezium.

10.   Find the height of the trapezium.

11.   What is half the total length of the two parallel sides?

12.   What is the area?

Make and complete the table below.

Name of shape.	Length of base.	Height	Area
Rectangle			
Triangle			
Parallelogram			
Trapezium			

Shapes Which Balance

Put a pencil on the desk and place a small triangle against it. Then place the second small triangle on the other side of the pencil so that the two triangles balance each other. Move the triangles to different positions so that they still balance. The balance lines may point in any direction.

When a shape balances on each side of a straight line it is said to be *symmetrical.*

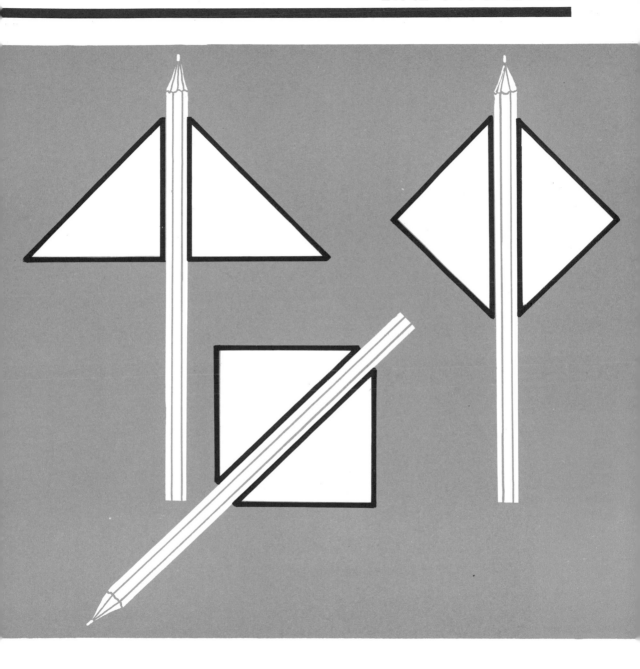

Shapes which Balance

The shapes on the following four pages can be made symmetrical by adding further pieces of the tangram. On these two pages we see how the large and small triangles can be used to make different symmetrical patterns. The shapes on the other four pages show only one balance line (the dotted line), but there are many other possible balance lines as the diagrams on this page show.

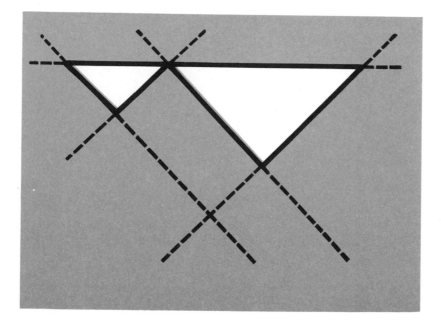

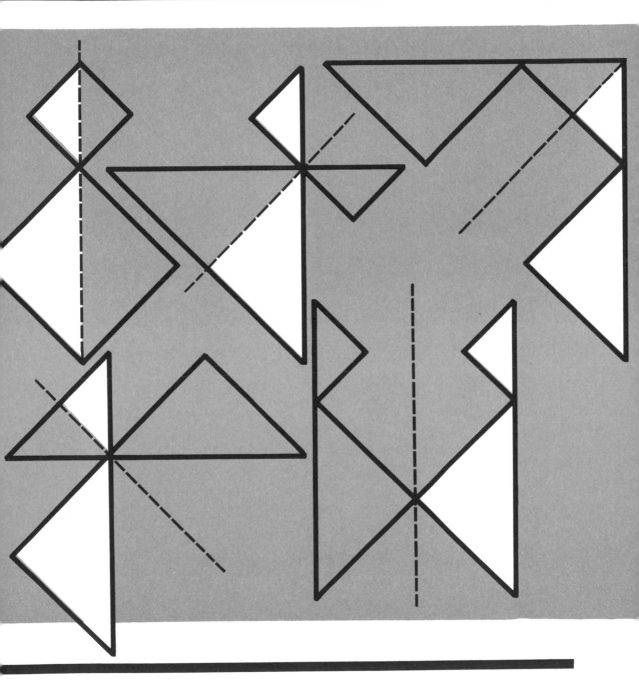

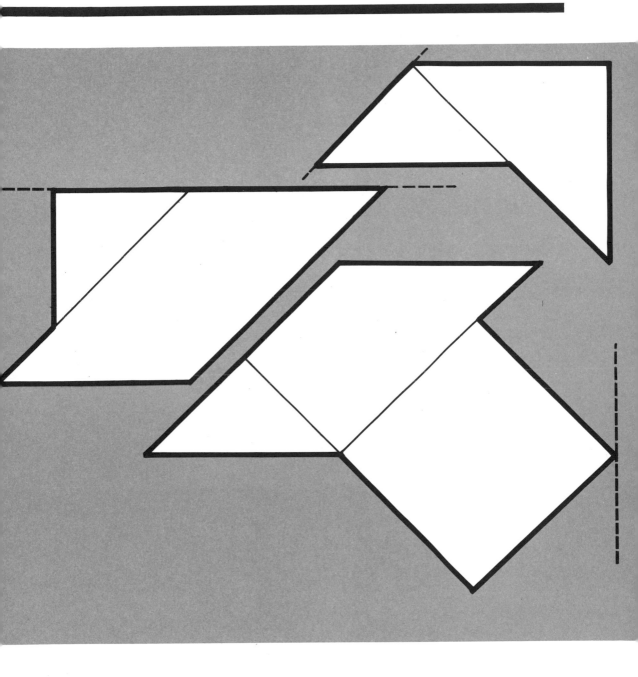

Symmetry

Make the shapes on the following four pages, and then place your pencil along the balance lines, to show how the shapes are symmetrical.

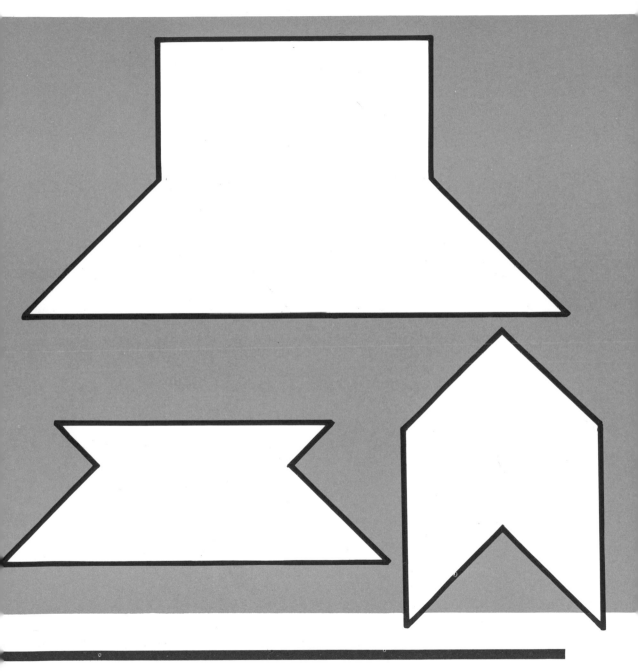

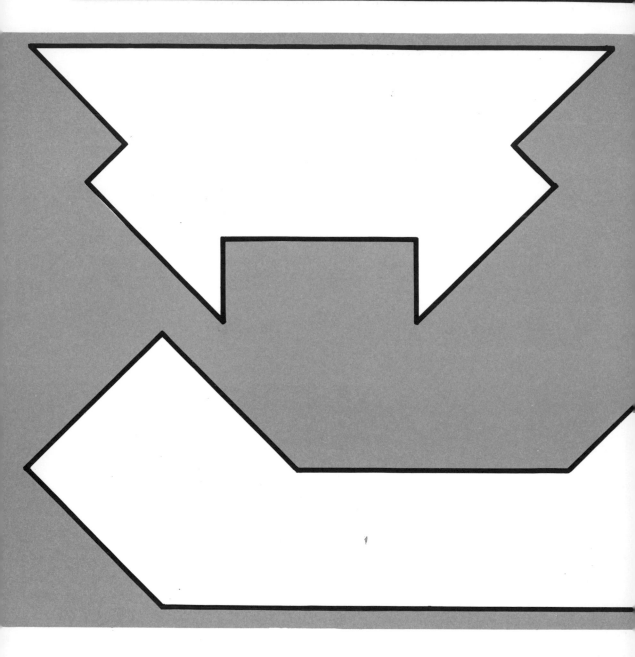

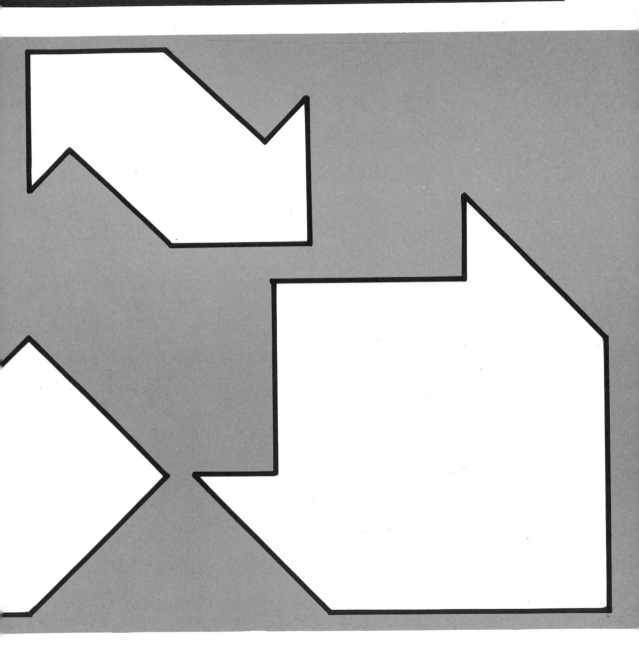

Identical Shapes and Similar Shapes

Shapes which are exactly alike will fit perfectly one on top of the other. Such shapes are *identical* with each other. They are *congruent.* Shapes which are like each other but which are different in size are said to be *similar.* The two top triangles opposite are identical or *congruent.* They will fit over each other exactly.

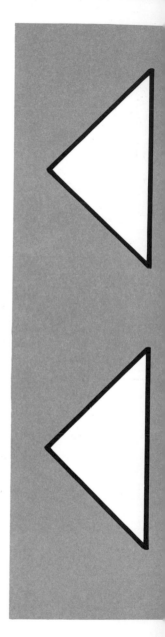

The two bottom triangles opposite are *similar.* Although these triangles are different in size, they are like each other. You will see that they have the same sized angles.

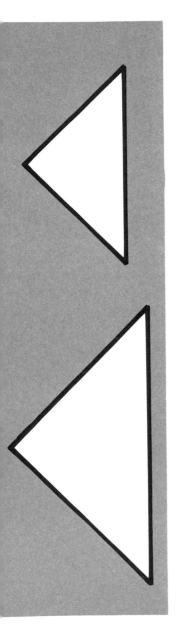

Congruent and Similar Shapes

1.   Place the large square on your desk. Build a square which is *identical* to it, and find a square (or build one) which is *similar* to it.

2.   Place the small triangle on your desk. How many *similar* triangles can you build, if you are allowed to choose from all seven pieces for each new triangle?

3.   Place the small square on your desk. How many *similar* squares can you build choosing from all seven pieces for each new square? Show on your drawing how each square was made.

4.   Place the parallelogram on your desk. Using each piece only once, build two more parallelograms, one of which is *congruent*, and the other *similar*.

Similar Shapes

Take each of these shapes in turn. First build the shape and then, using some of the remaining pieces, build a *similar* shape.

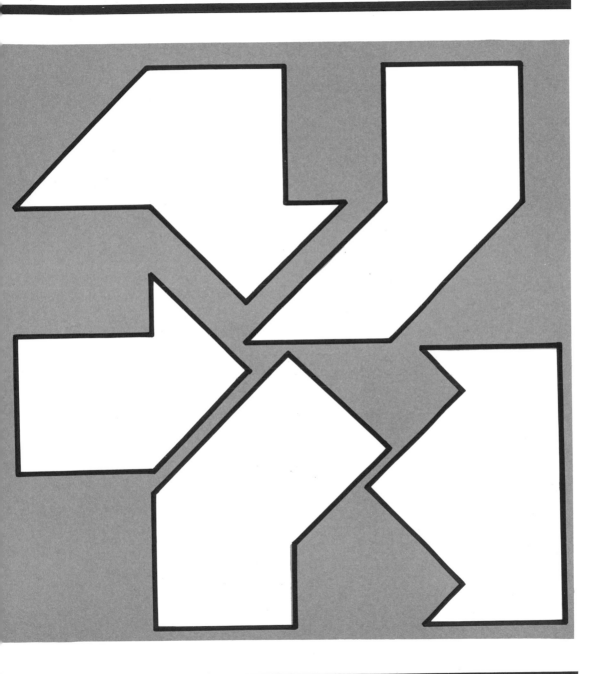

Congruent Shapes

Take each of the shapes on the next page in turn. First build the shape and then, using some of the remaining pieces, build a shape which is *identical* to the first one: the two shapes will then be *congruent*.

Using each piece once only, build three *congruent* parallelograms. Show that the three parallelograms are *congruent* by placing one on top of the other. Make as many parallelograms as you can, which are *similar* to the one in the puzzle, choosing from all seven pieces for each new parallelogram. Some parallelograms may appear to be *similar* when this is not so.

To test parallelograms for *similarity*, see if their diagonals lie along the same line. The two parallelograms on this page are *similar* because when one is placed on the other their diagonals lie along the same line.

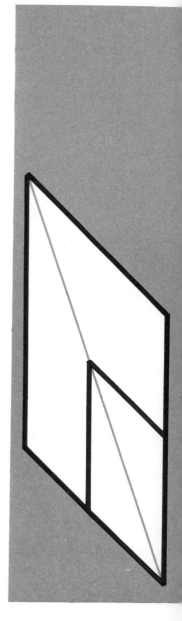

Some Difficult Shapes to Make

You must use all seven pieces of the tangram when making the shapes on this and the following pages. How many of these shapes can you make? Solutions to the problems on these two pages may be found on pages 78 and 79.

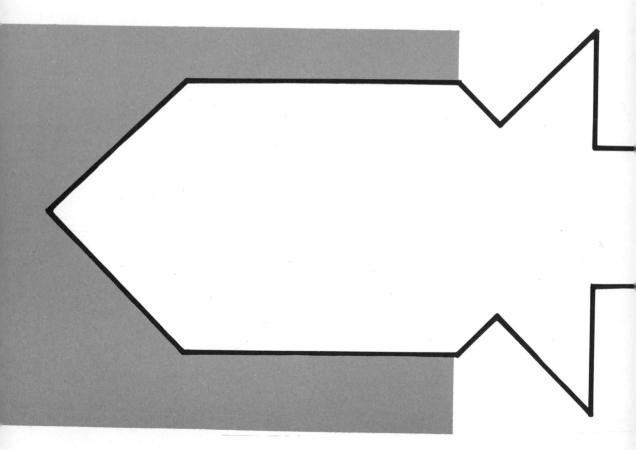

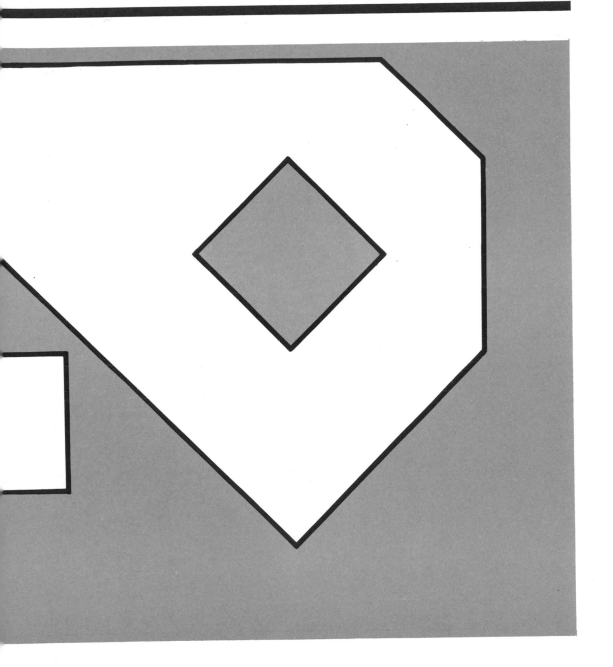

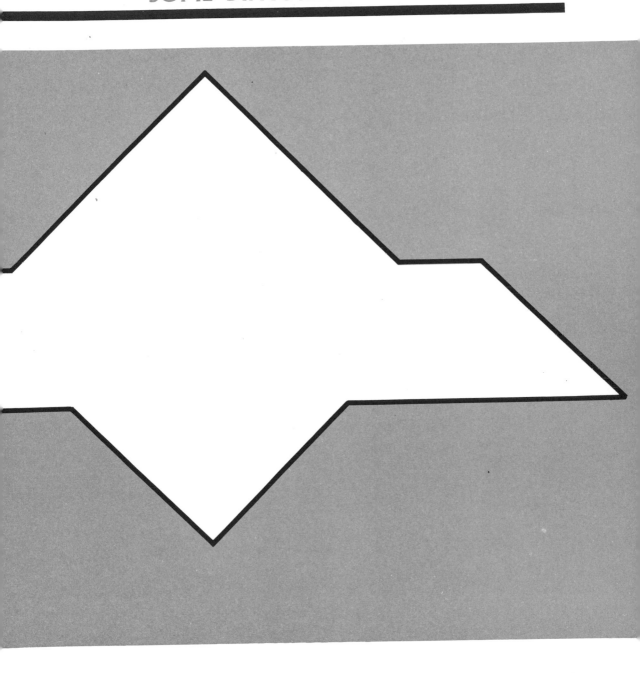

SOME DIFFICULT SHAPES MADE EASY

Solution to pages 74 and 75

DID YOU GET IT RIGHT?

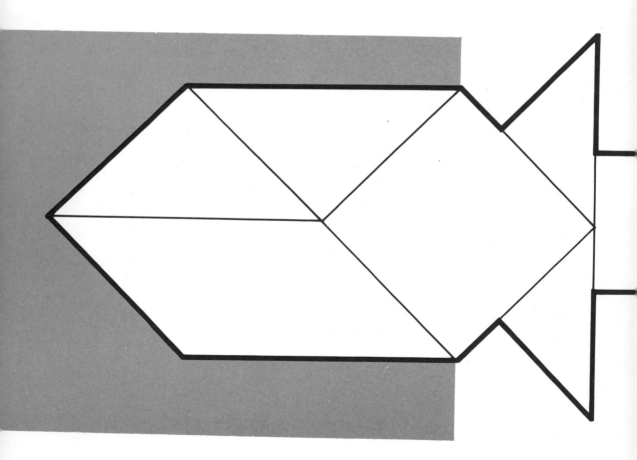

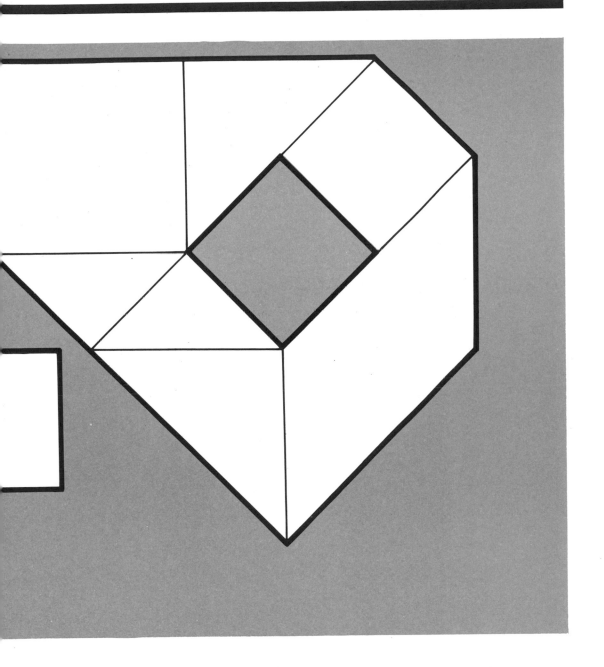

Some Basic Shapes Made Easy

Arrange the seven pieces of the Tangram to make three separate shapes as shown below. By studying the position of these three shapes carefully, and by moving them as one piece, many of the more difficult constructions can easily be completed.

Rectangle

Triangle

Right-angled Trapezium

Parallelogram

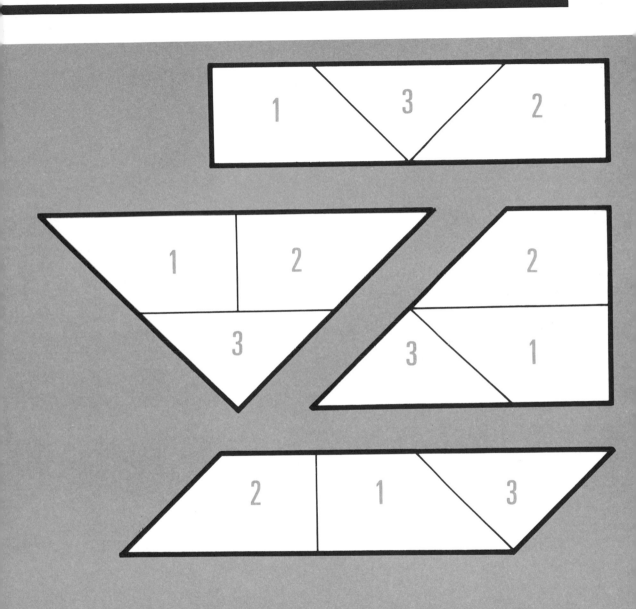